SUPERBUGS AND PANDEMICS

BY EMILY SOHN

ILLUSTRATED BY EDUARDO GARCIA

CAPSTONE PRESS
a capstone imprint

Published by Capstone Press, an imprint of Capstone.
1710 Roe Crest Drive
North Mankato, Minnesota 56003
capstonepub.com

Library of Congress Cataloging-in-Publication Data
Names: Sohn, Emily, author.
Title: Superbugs and pandemics : a max axiom super scientist adventure / Emily Sohn.
Description: North Mankato : Capstone Press, 2022. | Series: Max axiom and the society of super scientists | Includes bibliographical references and index. | Audience: Ages 8-11 | Audience: Grades 4-6
Summary: "A new disease has reared its ugly head. People are getting very sick with high fevers and an itchy rash. Even worse, it seems to be spreading quickly to several major cities around the world. What is this new disease, and why is it spreading so fast? It's up to Max Axiom and the Society of Super Scientists to find out! In this nonfiction graphic novel, young readers can follow the team as they go on an exciting, fact-filled adventure to learn how diseases work, why pandemics and superbugs are so dangerous, and things they can do to help stop the spread of deadly disease"-- Provided by publisher.
Identifiers: LCCN 2021033322 (print) | LCCN 2021033323 (ebook) | ISBN 9781663959201 (hardcover) | ISBN 9781666322767 (paperback) | ISBN 9781666322774 (pdf) | ISBN 9781666322798 (kindle edition)
Subjects: LCSH: Drug resistance in microorganisms--Juvenile literature. | Epidemics--Juvenile literature.
Classification: LCC QR177 .S63 2022 (print) | LCC QR177 (ebook) | DDC 616.9/041--dc23
LC record available at https://lccn.loc.gov/2021033322
LC ebook record available at https://lccn.loc.gov/2021033323

Editorial Credits
Editor: Aaron Sautter; Designer: Brann Garvey; Media Researcher: Morgan Walters; Production Specialist: Laura Manthe

All internet sites appearing in back matter were available and accurate when this book was sent to press.

TABLE OF CONTENTS

THE SOCIETY OF SUPER SCIENTISTS

MAX AXIOM

After years of study, Max Axiom, the world's first Super Scientist, knew the mysteries of the universe were too vast for one person alone to uncover. So Max created the Society of Super Scientists! Using their superpowers and super-smarts, this talented group investigates today's most urgent scientific and environmental issues and learns about actions everyone can take to solve them.

LIZZY AXIOM

NICK AXIOM

SPARK

THE DISCOVERY LAB

Home of the Society of Super Scientists, this state-of-the-art lab houses advanced tools for cutting-edge research and radical scientific innovation. More importantly, it is a space for Super Scientists to collaborate and share knowledge as they work together to tackle any challenge.

Great workout, Lizzy!

You too, Max. It feels so good to take care of myself.

Hi, Nick. What's happening?

BUZZ! BUZZ!

Max! Lizzy! Did you hear the news? Doctors have identified a new disease. It's popped up in several places around the world.

What else do we know?

The illness causes a variety of symptoms. They include an itchy rash, tingly hands and feet, cough, fever, and exhaustion. Tests aren't showing any known disease.

DISEASE DEFINITIONS

Scientists use a variety of words to describe the spread of diseases.

Epidemic: An increase in the number of cases of a disease above the normal rate in a population.

Outbreak: An epidemic in a limited geographic area.

Pandemic: An epidemic that has spread into several countries. It usually affects large numbers of people.

We need to get to the bottom of this illness—and quickly.

To stop this disease, it will help to understand what diseases are and how they spread.

Diseases start with germs.

Germs include viruses, bacteria, and parasites. Another word for germs is pathogens.

When pathogens get in our bodies, they try to multiply. Viruses need to get inside our cells to make copies of themselves. As they spread through our bodies, we can get sick.

Our immune systems fight back with specialized cells that look for signs of infection. Much of the time, immune cells win, and we never even know the pathogen was there.

In the mid-1300s, a disease called the bubonic plague swept through Europe.

By the time these ships arrived in Italy with sick sailors, the illness had already struck India, China, Egypt, and other countries.

The plague was a terrible disease. It was also called the Black Death. It ended up killing nearly one-third of the people in Europe.

Scientists now know that the plague is caused by bacteria. This germ can travel in the air when infected people cough. It can also get into people through bites from fleas, which bite infected rats.

Today we have a vaccine for measles. But back then, there was no way to prevent it.

Measles is very contagious. Each person who has it infects an average of 12 to 18 others. And it can be deadly.

Measles, smallpox, and other diseases took a terrible toll on the Native nations. Experts believe up to 90% of Native people died after Columbus arrived in 1492, and most of them died from disease.

How awful.

Yikes.

CONTAGIOUS STATS

Some diseases spread more easily than others. R0 is the term scientists use to describe how contagious a disease is. The R0 number shows the average number of other people that may get a disease from an infected person.

1918 flu: R0 = 1–2

Ebola virus: R0 = 1.5–2.5

Measles: R0 = 12–18

SARS: R0 = 1–2.75

Smallpox: R0 = 5–7

COVID-19: R0 = 2–3 (estimated)

From 1918 through 1919, the flu infected one-third of the world's population.

More than 50 million people died, including a lot of young people.

To slow the spread, a lot of schools held classes outside. Germs couldn't spread between people as easily outdoors.

We've learned some ways diseases have spread out of control. Let's see how the new illness compares to these examples from the past.

I have work to do at the lab. I'll meet you there later.

THE FLU

Influenza is the name of the virus that causes the flu. Many people get a flu shot in the fall or winter. Influenza comes in many forms, called strains. Often, the virus mutates, or changes into a new strain. Each year, scientists try to predict which strains will spread. They create a new vaccine each year that helps the body fight off those strains.

A rain forest? Don't we need to go help the patients?

It'll make sense in a moment. Meet Jen. She's a biologist.

Animals get sick with viruses and other pathogens, just like people do.

Right. Those diseases can wipe out entire species.

Sometimes, diseases can spread from animals to people. These are called **zoonotic** diseases.

There are many diseases that have spread from animals to people.

SWINE FLU

BIRD FLU

WEST NILE VIRUS

LYME DISEASE

EBOLA VIRUS

Some of those illnesses have caused serious outbreaks, epidemics, and pandemics.

Human activity is making zoonotic diseases more common. As people move deeper into animal habitats, there are more opportunities for diseases to spread.

Maybe animals had something to do with what happened to Elliot.

Someone could have been exposed to something that was contaminated by the new virus.

Then when they traveled home, they were likely near other people along the way. That would allow the virus to spread.

We have a lot of clues. Let's go share what we've learned with Nick.

COVID-19

The COVID-19 pandemic was first identified in China in late 2019. The virus rapidly spread all over the world. Countries used many strategies to try to stop the virus from infecting more people, including quarantines, mask orders, and contact tracing.

Vaccines are another important strategy for battling pandemics. Vaccines train the immune system to recognize diseases.

Vaccines can cause some side effects. But they protect people from serious illnesses. When viruses and bacteria can't infect new hosts, they can't spread easily.

It's smart to get your flu shot now, Lizzy. Flu season is about to start.

Some vaccines work by delivering parts of an inactive virus into our bodies. Others use harmless DNA from viruses. There are other methods too.

It can take many years to develop a vaccine. We still don't have vaccines for many illnesses.

Less than a year after the COVID-19 pandemic started, a vaccine was available. Scientists created it in record time.

I'll see you two later. I have an appointment with the TV news.

MORE ABOUT PANDEMICS

In 2020, the COVID-19 pandemic began to spread around the world. More than 180 million people got sick from the virus, which causes high fevers, coughing, loss of taste and smell, and other symptoms. By the fall of 2021, more than 4.5 million people had died around the world, including nearly 700,000 in the United States.

The COVID-19 pandemic shut down much of the world. Governments in many countries ordered people to stay home for weeks or months. When people were allowed to travel again, there were rules about wearing masks and staying apart from others.

The COVID-19 shutdowns caused a lot of hardships for people. Businesses closed. Millions of people lost their jobs. Millions of children had to stay home from school. A lot of people felt lonely and depressed. Experts argued about whether closing everything was worse than the virus. But others thought that many more people could have died without the restrictions. There were no easy answers.

The 1918 influenza pandemic was the most severe pandemic before COVID-19. An estimated 500 million people got infected with it. That was a third of all the people living on Earth! More than 50 million died around the world from the 1918 flu, including about 675,000 in the United States.

Scientists made vaccines for COVID-19 in record time. A lot of vaccines take many years to create. But several effective COVID-19 vaccines were ready in less than a year.

There are millions of types of viruses and bacteria in the world. Most don't make us sick. Many live in and on us at all times.

Every year, drug-resistant superbugs infect nearly 3 million people in the United States.

GLOSSARY

antibiotic (an-tee-bye-OT-ik)—a drug that kills bacteria and is used to cure infections and disease

contagious (kuhn-TAY-juhs)—carrying or spreading a disease from person to person

DNA (dee-en-AY)—the material in body cells that carries instructions to make a living thing and keep it working; DNA stands for deoxyribonucleic acid.

host (HOHST)—a living thing or cell that serves as a home or source of food for another living thing, such as a parasite, virus, or bacteria

immunity (ih-MYOO-ni-tee)—being able to resist or fight off disease

mutate (MYOO-tayt)—to change

pathogen (PATH-uh-jen)—a microorganism that causes disease

saliva (suh-LYE-vuh)—the clear liquid in your mouth produced by glands under the tongue and in the jaw

species (SPEE-sheez)—a group of plants or animals that share common characteristics

strain (STRAYN)—a bacteria or virus that causes symptoms similar to another but has unique characteristics

superbug (SOO-per-buhg)—a bacteria that has become resistant to common antibiotic medications

symptom (SIMP-tuhm)—a sign, such as a cough or a fever, that a person has an illness or is infected

vaccine (vak-SEEN)—a medicine that prevents a disease

zoonotic disease (zoh-on-OT-ik di-ZEEZ)—a disease caused by a germ that spreads from animals to people

READ MORE ////

Farndon, John. *Plague! Epidemics and Scourges Through the Ages.* Minneapolis: Lerner Publishing Group, Inc., 2017.

Platt, Richard and John Kelly. *The Germ Lab: The Gruesome Story of Deadly Diseases.* New York: Kingfisher, 2020.

Throp, Clair. *The Horror of the Bubonic Plague.* North Mankato, MN: Capstone Press, 2018.

INTERNET SITES

Biology for Kids: Epidemics and Pandemics
ducksters.com/science/biology/epidemics_and_pandemics.php

The History of Pandemics
timeforkids.com/g56/history-pandemics/

Outbreaks, Epidemics, and Pandemics
kidsboostimmunity.com/outbreaks-epidemics-and-pandemics

INDEX

ABOUT THE AUTHOR

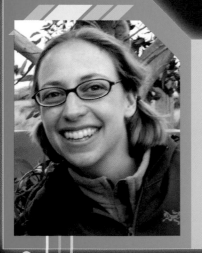

Emily Sohn is a freelance journalist in Minneapolis who covers mostly health, science, the environment, and adventure for both kids and grown-ups. Her work has appeared in *The New York Times*, *National Geographic*, *Nature*, *The Washington Post*, and many other publications. Assignments have taken Emily to exotic locations around the globe, including Cuba, Fiji, and the Peruvian Amazon.